EUSTON TO HARROW & WEALDSTONE

Keith Scholey

MP Middleton Press

Cover picture: Empty stock from Euston runs over one of the two electrified lines, as it approaches Primrose Hill Tunnel in July 1958. The locomotive is ex-LMS 2-6-2T no. 40070. (B.Morrison)

This book is dedicated to William Arthur Roberts.

Published October 2002

ISBN 1 901706 89 3

© Middleton Press, 2002

Design Deborah Esher

Published by
> *Middleton Press*
> *Easebourne Lane*
> *Midhurst, West Sussex*
> *GU29 9AZ*

Tel: 01730 813169
Fax: 01730 812601

Printed & bound by Biddles Ltd,
> *Guildford and Kings Lynn*

INDEX

ACKNOWLEDGEMENTS

    I greatly appreciate the help given by the photographers shown in the credits. Thanks go to the folks at the Camden Local Studies Centre, the Brent Archive and at Harrow Library for assistance rendered and also to Mr Richard Casserley for providing many of the views in this book. I should also like to thank Helen Roberts for the tedious proof reading and Godfrey Croughton for providing the ticket copies. I am also grateful to Jim Connor, John Gillham and Dennis Lovett for reading the text and to Vic Mitchell for adding many facts.

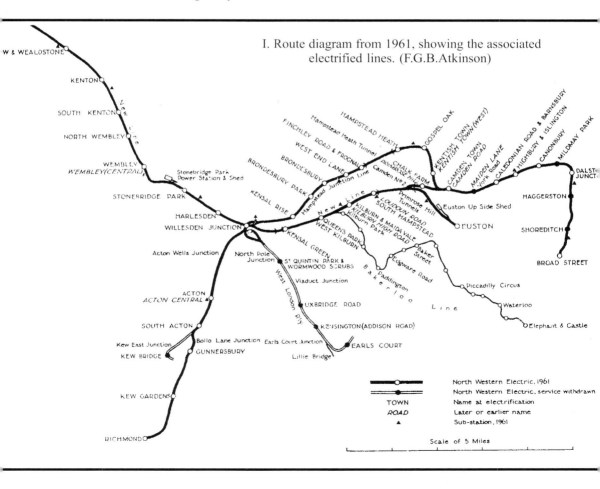

I. Route diagram from 1961, showing the associated electrified lines. (F.G.B.Atkinson)

GEOGRAPHICAL SETTING

The route runs north west from Euston for about a mile, then turns to run west to avoid running into the 'Northern Heights'. The Primrose Hill tunnels take the line under an extension of this high ground. After this the line turns south west. At Kensal Green a covered way takes the line through another area of high ground and after Willesden Junction the north west orientation is again picked up. Near Stonebridge Park the River Brent is crossed. The underlying ground is London Clay. Consecutively the London boroughs of Camden, Brent, Ealing and Harrow are passed.

II. Gradient profile

HISTORICAL BACKGROUND

The London & Birmingham Railway, the southern section of which forms the subject of this book, was London's first main line. Indeed in many ways it was the railway which impressed on the public that the age of the iron horse had truly arrived. Before this railways were obscure northern heavy freight carriers, such as the Stockton & Darlington, no doubt vital to the economy and technically amazing, but hardly world changing stuff. Or else they were penny-ha'penny affairs of mass transport, like the London & Greenwich of 1836, locally important but isolated. The London & Birmingham was different because it established the railways as a system- the multipurpose transportation network, for goods and passengers, over long and short distance. It didn't set out to do this however.

Initially the purpose of the L&B was to deliver the industrial produce of the Midlands (and the North West via the Grand Junction and London & Manchester Railways) to the huge domestic market of the capital. Long distance passenger traffic was thrown in, firstly as a sop to the public interest (the land needed for the railways was taken under state regulated compulsory purchase), and secondly, as was almost always the case with American companies, as a form of advertisement for its freight services. Short distance passenger traffic figured nowhere on the L&B's wants list.

When the London & Birmingham Railway was authorised by Act of Parliament of 6 May 1833, the London end was set at Camden. It has been stated that this was the intended terminus- Euston being a mere afterthought. This

was not so. The previous year the full line (i.e. including Euston) had been rejected by Parliament, presumably because of the disruption to the built-up area south of Camden it would cause, and a compromise line, excluding Euston put forward and found satisfactory. Yet even while the first sod was being turned at Chalk Farm in the Spring of 1834, negotiations to buy land around Euston Square were taking place. Agreement to use stationary steam engines to pull trains up what was to become known as Camden Bank, thus minimising noise and smoke pollution, made it easier to pass an extension to Euston the following year. Even so Camden must always have been foremost in the builders' minds: as the premier goods depot of the LNWR it was to occupy more land than Euston, and probably yielded more revenue.

The first section of the London & Birmingham, from Euston to Boxmoor (now Hemel Hempstead) was opened on 20 July 1837, with completion through to the 'second city' in the autumn of the following year. At this time the first station out of Euston was at Harrow. Despite expectations, demand for short distance service rapidly grew and by the time the London & Birmingham was incorporated into the London & North Western Railway in 1846, stations had been added at Willesden and Wembley. Not long after, stops were added at Camden (later known as Chalk Farm), and Kilburn. Suburban services however remained skimpy until the opening of a new bore at Primrose Hill in 1879 dramatically improved capacity by providing four tracks all the way from Euston to Watford. New stations were opened at Loudoun Road (now South Hampstead) and Queens Park. Despite these developments the London suburban services of the North Western at the turn of the century appeared rather mean compared to those of, say, the Great Northern.

Although the Euston line started with virtually no short distance services, it was to end up with one of the best served and systematically planned suburban services in London. That this was so was largely due to what may be termed the North Western renaissance. Around the turn of the century the LNWR seems to have had a sudden attack of the guilts. Here was 'the Premier Line' (as it advertised itself) with perhaps the best dividends of any pre-war company, yet with an infrastructure shabby and out-of-date. A station renewal programme was implemented. This was followed by the New Lines scheme, which was to be perhaps the most well-integrated suburban traffic programme ever implemented on this country's railways.

The first Act of 26 July 1907 authorised the LNWR to build a double track railway running parallel to its existing four-track line between Euston and Watford Junction. For the first seven or so miles the new line was to be north/east of the existing formation, crossing over to the west just south of Wembley. Electric throughout, the new line would be exclusively for suburban traffic. The electrification was at 600 volts DC, using the four rail system.

There were soon complications. In 1909 the LNWR took over management of the North London Railway, and it was decided to link electrification of this line to the existing scheme. Then the London Electric Railway got into the act with a projected extension of its Bakerloo line up to Queens Park.

The new line opened in stages: from Willesden to Harrow on 15 June 1912; and north to Watford early the following year. Bakerloo trains arrived at Queens Park on 11 February 1915, being extended to Willesden on 10 May. On 16 April 1917 the Willesden to Watford section was electrified (steam traction previously being used as a temporary stopgap). The First World War had slowed construction, so it wasn't until 10 July 1922 that public services over the entire line from Euston to Watford could be commenced.

Upon the grouping in 1923, the LNWR became part of the London Midland & Scottish Railway, which in turn formed the London Midland Region of British Railways upon nationalisation in 1948.

Overhead electrification at 25,000 volts AC was part of the modernisation of the main lines in 1964-66, but there was first a short period of diesel operation following the end of steam.

Sectorisation of BR in the mid-1980s resulted in local services being branded Network SouthEast, while long distance trains became InterCity. The "Harlequin Line" was a short-lived name for the DC route.

As a prelude to privatisation, local trains became part of North London Railways in 1994, which was given the meaningless name of Silverlink Trains following a 7½ year franchise being awarded to the National Express Group on 2nd March 1997. One week later, the Virgin Rail Group obtained a 15 year franchise for main line services from Euston, this excluding the Caledonian sleepers.

PASSENGER SERVICES

The table below indicates the number of trains from Euston calling at Harrow in sample years over the first seven decades of the line.

	Weekdays	Sundays
1841	6	2
1850	10	4
1869	22	5
1907	41	13

The advent of electrification brought a greatly increased frequency, which has been maintained ever since. However, Bakerloo services ceased between Queens Park and Watford Junction in October 1982, when the four remaining trips were withdrawn. They were restored as far as Harrow & Wealdstone in 1984, at 15-minute intervals.

OLD EUSTON

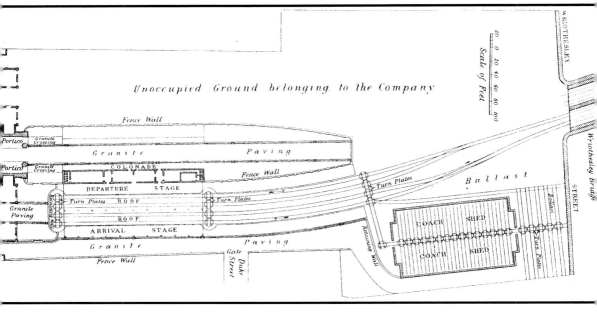

IIIa.   Because of the thoroughness of rebuilding, the current station and its predecessor are not directly comparable. It is helpful to view them as two separate entities- Old Euston and New Euston. The original layout of the station, as opened on 20th July 1837, reveals a simple two platform arrangement. These first two platforms were to form the core of the eastern group of platforms. One early plan showed platforms for the Great Western Railway occupying the vacant site to the west.

1.   The focal point of Old Euston was the Doric Arch, properly a Propylaeum, designed by Philip Hardwick senior. The simple classical lines of this grey granite monster made the station the first temple of transportation. With early Victorians hurrying to catch trains and a bevy of coaches, this is how the arch and its surroundings looked not long after construction was completed in May 1838. (K.A.Scholey coll.)

2.   In 1870 the Arch was already being overshadowed by later buildings. However the squat little lodges on the Euston Road were interesting additions that survive today. Destinations served by North Western trains are listed on the corner stones. (Illustrated London News)

IIIb.   This plan of 1914 gives an overview of Old Euston at its height. The approach began at Euston Road off to the left, went under the hotel, through the Arch, to deliver the passenger in the Great Hall. On either side of the Hall were two platform groups: the eastern section 1 to 7; and the western 8 to 13. The photographs are presented in that order.

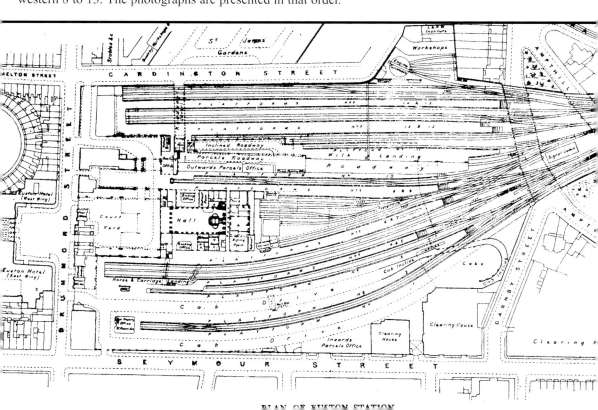

PLAN OF EUSTON STATION

3.   Added between the two Euston Road lodges in 1921 is the memorial to the LNWR railwaymen who died in the Great War. The white limestone obelisk, with its four bronze statues of servicemen is another modern day survivor. (K.A.Scholey coll.)

4.   The next item on the approach axis is this addition to the Euston Hotel, which wrecked the distant view of the arch seen in picture 2. Built in 1881 this Victorian monstrosity was thankfully swept away during the rebuilding. (K.A.Scholey coll.)

5.   The rear view of the hotel was less offensive. The original buildings of 1839, designed by Philip Hardwick senior, are to either side. There were originally two hotels, the Euston and the Victoria, which were the first railway owned hotels in the world. (K.A.Scholey coll.)

6.   A close up view of the Arch around 1925 shows it to be thoroughly hemmed in, and the lodges patched and untidy. The letters had been engraved above the entrance in 1870: this was really gilding the lily - what other station could it have been? (K.A. Scholey coll.)

7.   Through the Arch was a cobbled yard. Seen here around 1905, the outside of the Great Hall is in front of us, whilst to the right is a building partly dating back to 1836. Inside the Hall may have been good architecture, but outside it was a bland façade. (K.A.Scholey coll.)

8.   In 1914 there were major alterations in the forecourt with a new glass and metal awning erected. In this November 1961 view, a little line of passengers waits to be picked up. (J.C.Gillham)

9.   The 1914 rebuilding included a new booking office situated in front of the Great Hall complex. The barrel vaulted roof and stone pilasters made this space quite fine in appearance, but the site made it rather cramped. (J.C.Gillham)

10.   The Great Hall, the grandest waiting room in Europe, was opened on 27th May 1849 and is seen here in 1953. Designed by P.C. Hardwick, it was hugely costly. Even so the materials used were substandard- the 'marble' columns were plaster. Behind the statue of George Stephenson is the LNWR Boer War memorial. (A.C.Ingram)

11.   At the top of the stairs was this statutary group. Like the tablets in the upper corners of the Great Hall representing LNWR towns, it was carved by John Thomas, who also worked on the Great Western Hotel at Paddington with Hardwick. With George Stephenson's statue, it can now be found at the National Railway Museum. (Illustrated London News)

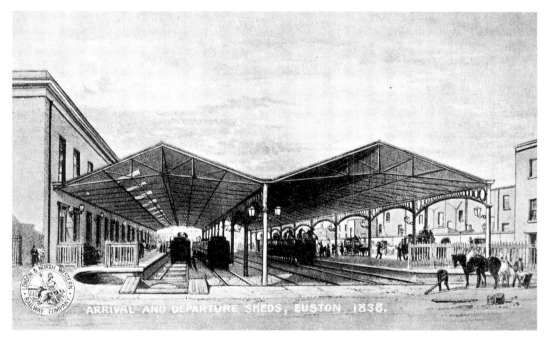

ARRIVAL AND DEPARTURE SHEDS, EUSTON 1838.

12.   This room, the Shareholders Meeting Room, was the true centre of Old Euston. This was what Euston, the LNWR and all Victorian railways were about making money. As befits the most important area in the station, it is highly ornate and richly decorated. It fell with the Great Hall. (Illustrated London News)

13.   The sparing design of the original two-span train shed was in complete contrast to noble dimensions of the Arch. The outer two tracks were for arrivals and departures, the inner pair for carriage storage. The departure platform (to the left) would later be extended and renumbered as 6, whilst the arrival platform was lost in transit. (K.A.Scholey coll.)

IIIc. Diagram from the early 1960s.

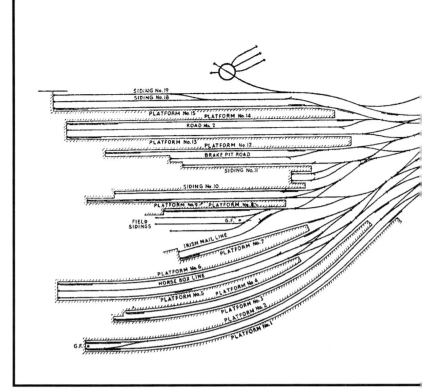

SIDING No. 19
SIDING No. 18
PLATFORM No. 15   PLATFORM No. 14
ROAD No. 2
PLATFORM No. 13   PLATFORM No. 12
BRAKE PIT ROAD
SIDING No. 11
SIDING No. 10
PLATFORM No. 9   PLATFORM No. 8
FIELD SIDINGS   G.F.
IRISH MAIL LINE
PLATFORM No. 7
PLATFORM No. 6
HORSE BOX LINE
PLATFORM No. 5   PLATFORM No. 4
PLATFORM No. 3
PLATFORM No. 2
PLATFORM No. 1
G.F.

14.   Platforms 1 and 2, seen here around 1905, were mostly used for arrivals. Electric lighting was installed that year. Although built in 1873, their roofing was clearly in the style of the original. The cab road is to the left. (K.A.Scholey coll.)

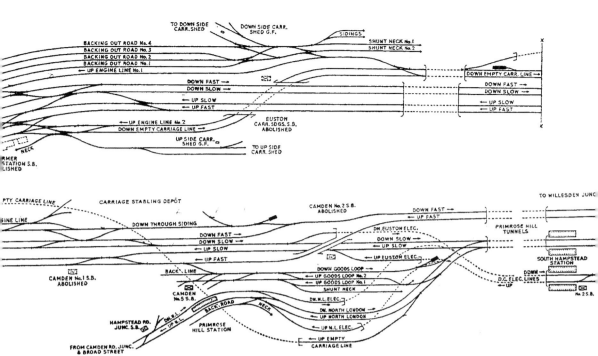

15.   Here we see the country end of the eastern group of platforms around 1930 as an electric train of Oerlikon stock leaves from platform 4. These trains provided the main Euston-Watford electric service from 1922 until their withdrawal in the late 1950s. Platforms 4 and 5 were added in 1891 and used by New Line electric trains. Electrically operated points and signals were installed as far as Camden in 1905. (K.A.Scholey coll.)

16. This 1963 view of the cab road exit makes an interesting comparison with picture 13. To the far right is the train arrival bureau, a late addition of 1951, whilst behind it is a squat building formerly in use as the lost property office. Average daily passengers were 300 in 1837, 60,000 in 1937 and 141,000 in 2002. (J.C.Gillham)

17. The entrance to the cab road was located round the corner in Eversholt Street. After passing over platforms 1 and 2 it descended via this steep ramp. The curvature of these platforms was a significant factor in the rebuilding. (J.C.Gillham)

18.   A mail train stands at platform 5 some time in the early 1960s. No. 45044 is a Black Five, the LMS's maid of all work. Its replacement lurks behind. This traditional scene was soon to vanish forever: when this shot was taken, rebuilding was about to begin. (R.S.Carpenter)

19.   Around the same time no. 46141 *The North Staffs Regiment* backs out of the station. The "Royal Scots" were built in the late 1920s for the through Euston to Scotland services, but were later downgraded to lighter duties. This is a rebuilt example. The lighter patch of brickwork marks where the Ampthill Square bridge stood until its removal in 1952. (R.S.Carpenter)

20.　　Platforms 9 and 10 were added in 1846 and adjoined the Great Hall complex, the side of which is to the right. Platform 9, known as "The York" from the destination of its earliest trains, was mostly used for parcels traffic.　(K.A.Scholey coll.)

21.　　One of the forgotten nooks of Old Euston is seen here in 1963. This yard was located between platform 10 and the western platforms (12 to 15). The building to the left is marked on the 1914 plan as Outwards Parcels Office and would appear to date from the 1840s. (J.C.Gillham)

22.   The appearance of the western platforms was somewhat different. Platforms 12 to 15 lay beneath a massive girder roof finished in 1892. Traditionally this was the main line departure side and is seen here around 1905. (K.A.Scholey coll.)

23.   This 1963 view was taken looking south from the end of platform 15. The north end of these platforms was a rather remote outpost. To the right is a small stationary boiler used for providing steam for carriage heating. (J.C.Gillham)

NEW EUSTON

24.   In 1961 scaffolding is up and demolition is imminent. Despite an outcry, the Arch was pulled down. The contractor numbered the stones, some of which have recently been found, and there is a suggestion again that the Arch should be rebuilt. (A.C.Ingram)

25.   While parts of the old station lingered elsewhere, by May 1963 the site of the eastern platforms had been largely cleared. The side of the Great Hall complex is to the left. (J.C.Gillham)

26.   The new station, an airport terminal look-alike, was designed by R.L.Moorcroft. The original model seen here is now at the National Railway Museum. End loading was possible at platforms 17 and 18, this facility being used by Motorail trains. (K.A.Scholey)

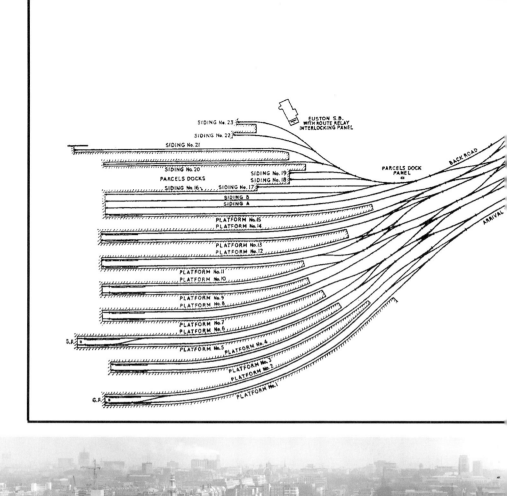

SIDING No. 23

SIDING No. 22

SIDING No. 21

EUSTON S.B.
WITH ROUTE RELAY
INTERLOCKING PANEL

SIDING No. 20

SIDING No. 19

PARCELS DOCKS

SIDING No. 18

PARCELS DOCK
PANEL

BACK ROAD

SIDING No. 16

SIDING No. 17

SIDING B

SIDING A

ARRIVAL

PLATFORM No. 15

PLATFORM No. 14

PLATFORM No. 13

PLATFORM No. 12

PLATFORM No. 11

PLATFORM No. 10

PLATFORM No. 9

PLATFORM No. 8

PLATFORM No. 7

PLATFORM No. 6

G.F.

PLATFORM No. 5

PLATFORM No. 4

PLATFORM No. 3

PLATFORM No. 2

G.F.

PLATFORM No. 1

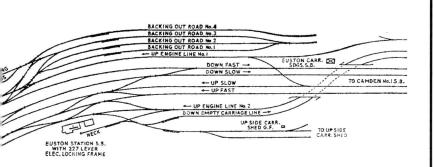

BACKING OUT ROAD No.4
BACKING OUT ROAD No.3
BACKING OUT ROAD No.2
BACKING OUT ROAD No.1
← UP ENGINE LINE No.1

DOWN FAST →
DOWN SLOW →

EUSTON CARR.
SDGS. S.B.

← UP SLOW
← UP FAST

TO CAMDEN No.1 S.B.

← UP ENGINE LINE No.2
DOWN EMPTY CARRIAGE LINE →

UP SIDE CARR.
SHED G.F.

TO UP SIDE
CARR. SHED

NECK

EUSTON STATION S.B.
WITH 227 LEVER
ELEC. LOCKING FRAME

IIId. The 1960s rebuilding brought the platforms almost into a straight row and rationalised the track work of the approaches.

(lower left)
27. New Euston was opened in stages: the platforms came into use from 1966, whilst the main concourse was officially opened by the Queen on 14th October 1968. This overview taken during the final stages of building probably dates from 1967. The bulk of Euston House, built as the headquarters of the LMS, can be seen at the top left. (K.A.Scholey coll.)

28. On the left no. 87001 prepares to lead the 09.35 to Inverness on 19th December 1979. The 87s and the earlier, almost identical, 86s were the motive power on 90% of express passenger workings out of Euston in the period 1965 to 1990. Augmented by class 90s they were still in use in 2002. (T.Heavyside)

29.   AM10 units (later known as class 310) provided the outer suburban services after their electrification. No. 310055 is seen here in 1975. Provided with an open layout but with slam doors, these trains seemed very clunky and old-fashioned by the time of their transfer to other routes in the late 1980s. (M.Turvey)

IIIe.   The post-2000 diagram shows mostly reversible lines. The subways were subsequently used by express trains.

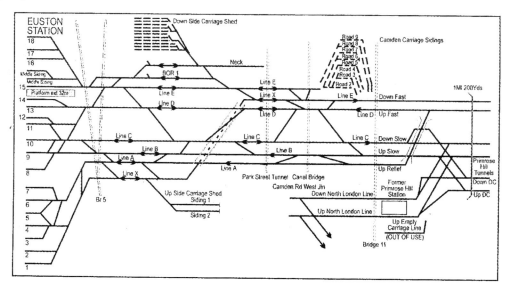

30.   Their replacements in 1990 were class 317s from the St.Pancras - Bedford line. These lovely sleek class 321s followed. Remodelling and resignalling of the approaches began in 1999 and was completed in September 2000. Thereafter operations were controlled from the new Wembley Signalling Centre. (M.Turvey)

NORTH OF EUSTON

31.   The area north of the station was a complex mass of junctions - all the platforms fed into the four running lines. In 1905 the area was overshadowed by the two huge girder bridges carrying the north and south sides of Ampthill Square over the lines. (K.A. Scholey coll.)

32.   By 1953 both bridges had been pulled down and No. 2 Box was shortly to follow. No. 1 Box controlled platforms 1-5 and the others were under the responsibility of this box, numbered 2. It had 282 levers (in two frames) and replaced one of 54 levers in 1891. A single new box with 227 miniature levers for electro-pneumatic operation was opened on 5th October 1952. (R.S.Carpenter)

33.   Heading north with the "Coronation Scot" not long after the introduction of the service in 1937, we see streamlined "Pacific" no. 6223 *Princess Alice* from the Hampstead Road bridge. The locomotive is in its original magnificent blue and silver livery. The "Coronations" (informally "Big Lizzies") were used on the top expresses between the late 1930s and the early 1960s. (C.L.Turner/R.M.Casserley)

Camden Bank

34.   Building a railway in the Victorian age was a truly Herculean task as can be seen here. This reproduction Bourne print issued by the LNWR as a postcard in 1905 shows the line north of Mornington Street in an advanced state of construction. The works are swarming with gangs of navvies, probably Irishmen. (K.A.Scholey coll.)

35.   Seventy years later, the view has changed in detail but the Park Street (now Parkway) bridge is common to both views. In the foreground, tracks used for empty stock workings pass below the running lines. On the right a suburban train passes the side of the Up Carriage Shed.
(K.A. Scholey coll.)

36.   After charging up the bank, we pass the side of the goods depot. This 1957 view shows the main shed as extended in the 1930s. With a few exceptions, which now form part of the famous Camden Market, the goods station complex was demolished after closure. (P.C.Wheeler)

37.   A major rail served customer at Camden was W & A Gilbey, distillers and spirit merchants. In this turn of the century engraving the extent of their premises can be seen. The goods shed is to the left, with the North London line running left to right beyond it. (K.A. Scholey coll.)

Camden Engine Shed

——————→

38.   The main attraction at Camden however was the Round House. This was originally built as shed for goods engines in 1847 at which date it is seen in this old engraving. The engines are more imagination than real.
(Illustrated London News)

39.   Designed by R.B.Dockray, the shed remained in use only until 1871, when it was converted for use as a warehouse for Gilbeys. Since 1964 it has been used off and on as an arts centre and is seen here the following year.
(J.C.Gillham)

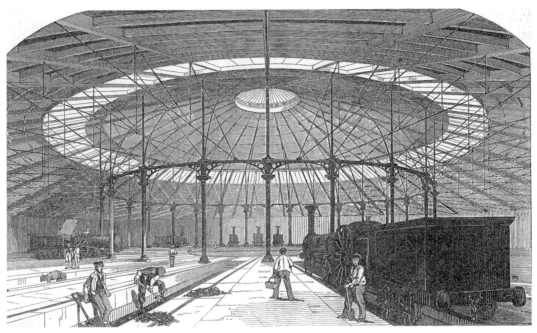

——————→

40.   An engine shed was located at Camden from the opening of the line. In the 1840s a new shed was built, as seen here around 1885. Unlike its contemporary the Round House, this was of conventional design and originally featured a prominent gable end. (K.A. Scholey coll.)

41.   In 1934 the shed was given a new flat roof, as seen here from the north during the final stages of construction on 29th June. The goods depot can be seen beyond the running lines to the left. (H.F.Wheeller)

42.   Camden was used almost exclusively by express passenger engines, such as this rather grimy "Big Lizzie", seen here in 1945 shortly before her streamlining was removed. Steam lasted until 1962. The diesels did not stay long however and the shed closed on 3rd January 1966. Carriage sidings occupy most of the site. (H.C.Casserley)

43.   An Oerlikon set clatters between the goods depot (well-filled yard to left) and the shed (sidewall to right) on 9th June 1945. Colour light signals replaced the semaphores the day after the photograph was taken. (H.C.Casserley)

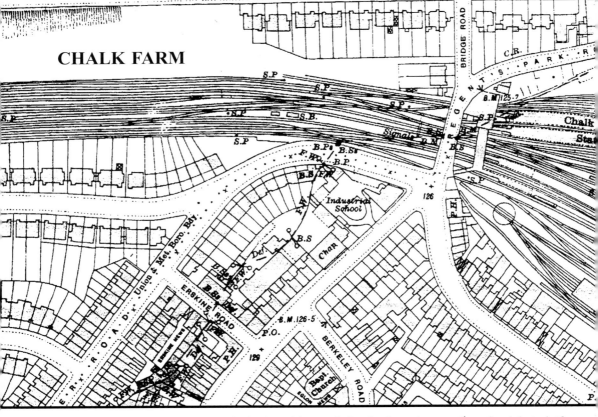

CHALK FARM

IV. The LNWR station here had a long history dating back to the opening of a ticket platform around 1844. Known as Camden, this was upgraded to full station status on 1st November 1851. Resited in 1852 and 1872, the station became Chalk Farm in 1876, and was closed on 10th May 1915. There was also a stop here on the North London line from 1851 to 1992, which was renamed Primrose Hill on 25th September 1950. This 1914 map shows the earlier layout with access to the platforms via tunnels.

44. The booking office building, dating from late 1871, served the North London and LNWR platforms and is seen here around 1905. The architect was Henry Woodhouse of the Engineers Office at Stafford, who also designed the old station at Roade. (K.A.Scholey coll.)

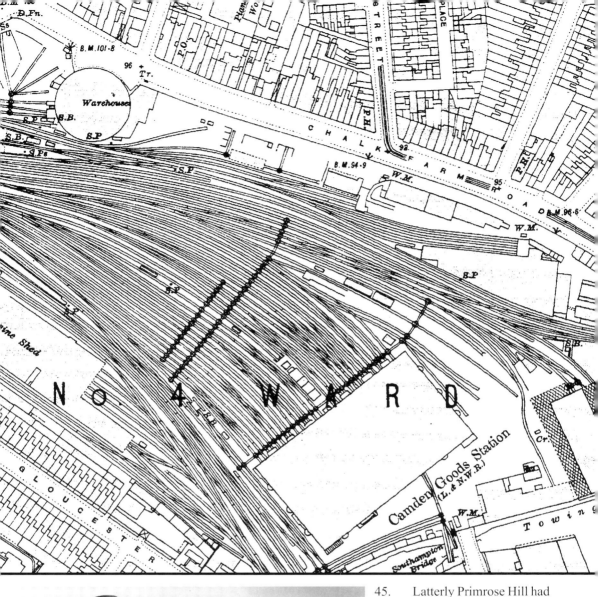

Warehouse

CHALK FARM ROAD

B.M.101·8

96

B.M.94·9

N O   4   W A R D

Camden Goods Station
(L. & N.W.R.)

G L O U C E S T E R

Southampton
Bridge

Towing

45.   Latterly Primrose Hill had only an irregular service of North London line trains. Around 1950 the front section had been reconstructed in the rather utilitarian fashion shown here. The main line platforms were long gone and the station closed officially on 28th September 1992, although the last train called on the 22nd. By that time there was only one stopping in each direction - Mondays to Fridays only - and it was between Liverpool Street. and Watford Junction. (J.C.Gillham)

PRIMROSE HILL TUNNELS

46.   Just after clattering through the junctions west of Primrose Hill station, we come to the first tunnel on the route. The ornate portal at the east end, seen here in its original 1836 condition, was designed by a Mr Budden (not one of the Stephensons as is often stated). 3492 ft long, it took eight million bricks to build. (K.A. Scholey coll.)

47.   Having passed through the tunnels we look back from Loudoun Road at the interesting but rather less picturesque western portals. Further tunnels were added to the original in 1879 and 1922 (the year before this picture was taken). The girder bridge carries the Great Central Railway lines bound for Marylebone. (K.A.Scholey coll.)

SOUTH HAMPSTEAD

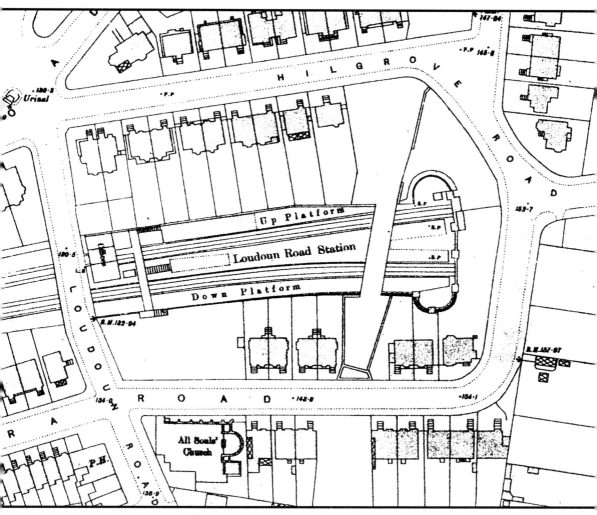

V.   This OS map of 1896 shows the station as it would have been when it opened on 2nd June 1879 with the original name Loudoun Road. The Great Central Railway's formation for its main line is in the process of being built crossing between the station and the tunnels. In 1922 platforms serving the New Line were added to the north.

48.	The clap-boarded booking office building was rather fine and with its Tudor style chimneys fitted in well with its upper-class surroundings. A similar example was once to be found at Wolverton in Buckinghamshire, but this too has vanished. (K.A.Scholey coll.)

49.	Temporarily closed in 1917, Loudoun Road reopened as South Hampstead on 10th July 1922. Looking west in the following year we can see the back of the booking office with the newly completed New Line platforms to the right. (K.A.Scholey coll.)

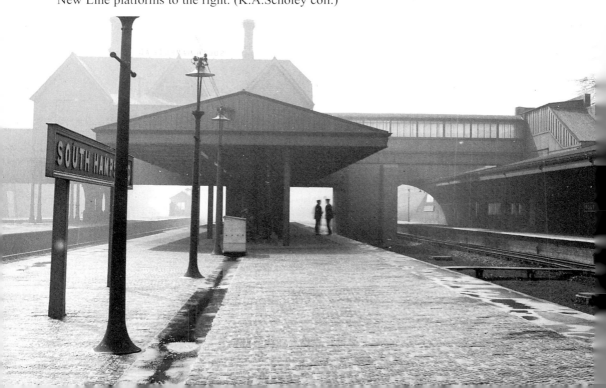

50.   The present entrance to the station could not be more of a contrast to the original. Dating from around 1970, it was carried out in best British Rail public lavatory style. However perhaps it is more suited to its current environment than its predecessor. (K.A.Scholey)

51.   At platform level the changes were just as drastic as above ground. The traditional canopies were swept away and replaced with bus shelters. Even the footbridge is modern. A typical throng of invisible people awaits the next train. (K.A.Scholey)

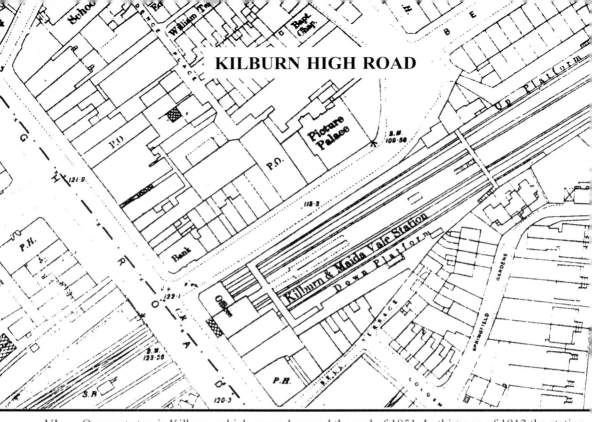

KILBURN HIGH ROAD

VI.   Our next stop is Kilburn, which opened around the end of 1851. In this map of 1912 the station will seem both familiar and somewhat strange to modern users. There is the current booking office on the High Road leading down via the footbridge to todays platforms. But at the other end of the platforms is another booking office and another footbridge! And there were two extra platforms too. The suffix "& Maida Vale" was added on 1st June 1875.

52.   The main (now only) entrance was on the High Road. Probably dating from 1879, it is seen here in 1902. The hefty glass and iron porch resembled that formerly outside Uxbridge Road station on the West London line. (K.A. Scholey coll.)

53.   A LNWR "Precursor" class 4-4-0 heading an express bound for Euston speeds under the High Road building in this turn of the century view. The "Precursors" were the North Westerns top-notch engines when introduced in 1904, but were soon downgraded. Another train, apparently of North London Railway stock, occupies the far platform. (K.A. Scholey coll.)

54.   A century later the scene on the High Road is still recognisable, however the façade of the station has undergone significant changes and is really little more than a hole in the wall between two shops. The station was closed between 1st January 1917 and 10th July 1922. Its name was changed from Kilburn & Maida Vale to Kilburn High Road on 1st August 1923. (K.A.Scholey)

55. As at South Hampstead, the old platform buildings have been replaced by bus shelters. Although only served by New Line electric trains since 1922, the platforms themselves are the originals of the 1850s; successive widenings of the line were to the south here. (K.A.Scholey)

56. The rear of the old station backs on to the platforms and is attached to the former booking office. The timber structure next to the house used to be part of the old footbridge. Awnings originally ran to just beyond the second lamppost - the remains of their stanchions can be clearly seen. (K.A.Scholey)

57.   Around the corner in Belsize Road are the original station buildings dating back to the 1850s. This elegant white stuccoed edifice, carried out in the then fashionable Italianate style, was once the stationmasters house and is now a private residence. (K.A.Scholey)

QUEENS PARK

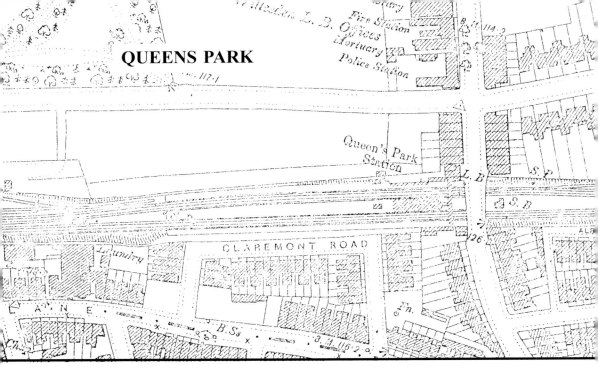

58.   The booking office building, seen here in early 1923, was built for the New Line/ Underground scheme but does not resemble any contemporary structure on the line. The front was tiled over in the 1970s. (London Transport)

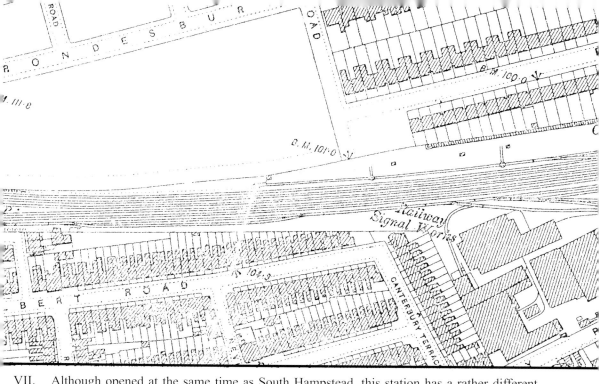

VII.   Although opened at the same time as South Hampstead, this station has a rather different history. In 1896 the station was a simple four platform job with a square brick booking office off to the north of the tracks.

59.   An early Underground train lurks under the substantial overall roof around 1930. Also evident is the broken edge of the old island platform. Interestingly there is no sign of access to the slow line platforms. (Stations UK)

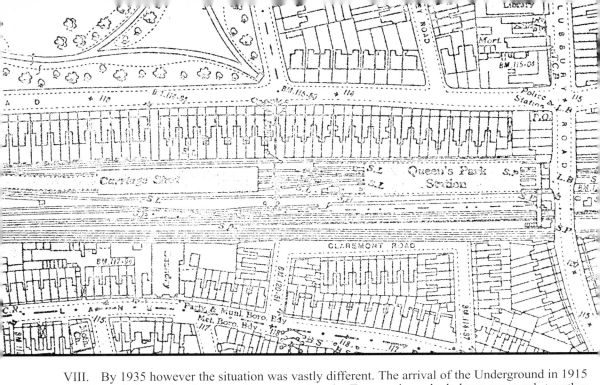

VIII. By 1935 however the situation was vastly different. The arrival of the Underground in 1915 transformed the station into a major transport node. Two carriage sheds have appeared, together with two more platforms serving the slow lines.

60. The slow line platforms (which are not in regular use) originally served the fast lines before these were rejigged to the south. In October 1964 the wires are up but the electrics are not yet running. This is an eastward view. (J.C.Gillham)

61. There are two carriage sheds at Queens Park used for stabling Bakerloo stock. Uniquely Bakerloo trains run right through the western depot, seen here in 1964. The raw bricks have since been decently covered up. (J.C.Gillham)

62.   The other carriage shed is to the east. On the right a 1972 stock Bakerloo Line train has just emerged from the Underworld. The BR southbound local line track is to the left of the depot, while the northbound is beyond the retaining wall on the right. (K.A.Scholey)

⎯⎯⎯⎯⎯⟶

63.   The station roof is a substantial bit of metalwork but surprisingly the platforms remain well lit and are rendered pleasant by hanging baskets. The centre tracks are for Bakerloo Line trains whilst the outer platforms are for Euston-Watford trains. (K.A.Scholey)

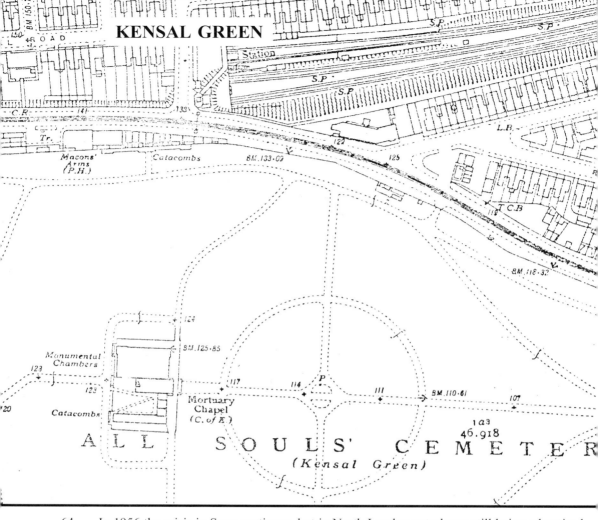

64.   In 1956 the crisis in Suez continues, but in North London petrol was still being advertised. Forty years old at this point the bespoke building on the corner of College Road and Harrow Road had already been altered, the door to the left being blocked up. (London Transport)

IX.   Opened on 1st October 1916, this station lies at the eastern end of the Kensal Green tunnels, and for the first five years or so was served only by Bakerloo trains. This is a 1935 map.

65.   The replacement for the building in the previous shot was completed in January 1981. With its timber cladding, brickwork and gables, it is an early example of the corporate BR style of the 1980s and 90s. (K.A.Scholey)

66.   The platforms remained essentially unaltered by the changes of the early 80s. Looking at the irregularities of the southbound platform canopy one rather thinks replacement is now a little overdue. (K.A.Scholey)

EAST OF WILLESDEN JUNCTION

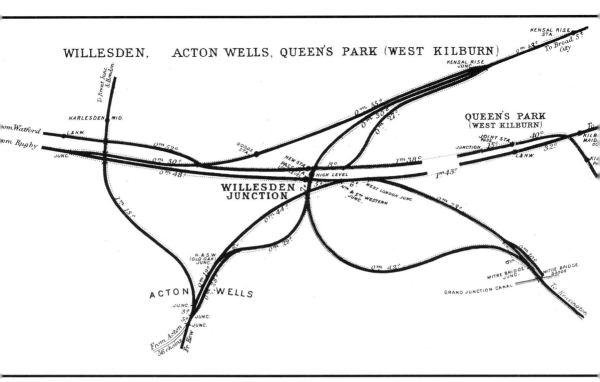

X.   Willesden Junction is best viewed as three distinct but linked stations: the High Level (covered in *Willesden Junction to Richmond*, *West London Line* and *North London Line* books by Middleton Press), the old main line or Low Level station and the New Station serving the Bakerloo and Euston-Watford line. This Railway Clearing House map dates from 1920.

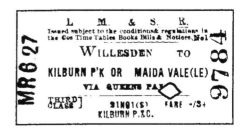

67.   We are now facing the east end of the current depot, which was built on the site of the old South Carriage sheds. Here the main line passes straight on to the left of the shed, whilst the New Line (just visible in the foreground) curves round to the right. (K.A.Scholey)

68.   Seen from Willesden Junction High Level station on 28th October 1980 is a class 501 set as it clatters past the side of the shed before entering the station. Here the New Line meets a short connecting spur (left) which runs up to the high level North London Line past an electricity sub-station. It is known as the City Loop Line. (J.C.Gilham)

WILLESDEN JUNCTION

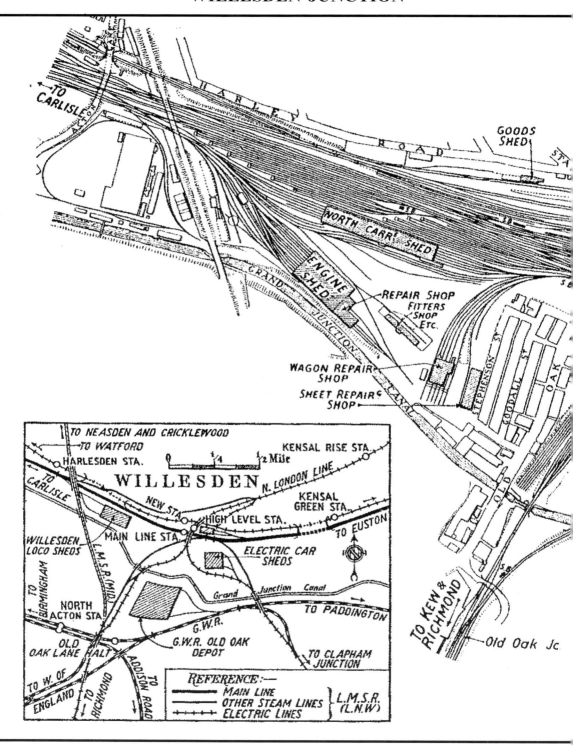

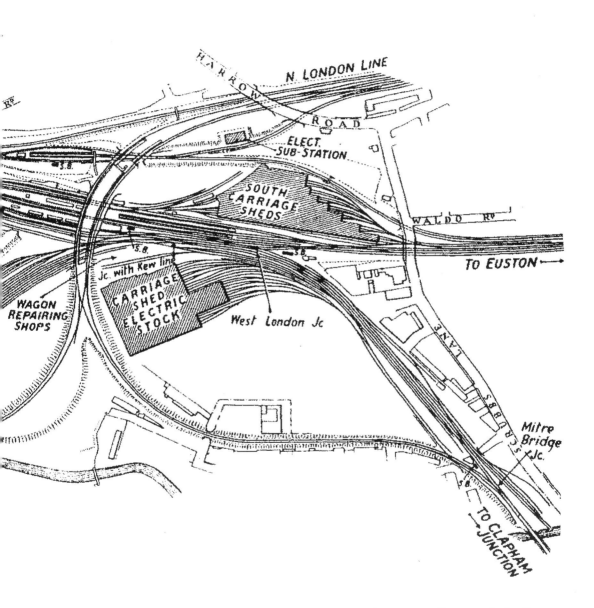

XI.   After passing through the Kensal Green Tunnels we head due west until we reach the first group of sidings. We are now entering an area of extensive railway development - this map of 1933 will provide a good guide to facilities here.

69.   Taking the main line station first: this is the booking office around the turn of the century. With its multi-coloured brickwork, this building was brought into use on 1st July 1891. On the side of the building can be seen one of the North Western's rather wordy signboards. (K.A.Scholey coll.)

70.   In a view from the same era, we see the main line platforms from west of the Old Oak Lane bridge. In most respects they were unaltered from their opening on 1st September 1866. The rear of the booking office can be seen to the left. (K.A. Scholey coll.)

71.   Willesden has seen only one notable accident. On 5th December 1910 a Broad Street-bound train slammed into the rear of a Watford to Euston local standing at platform 4. Two carriages telescoped killing five people and injuring over seventy more. An inquest concluded that the signalman had pulled the wrong lever by mistake. (K.A.Scholey coll.)

72.   This photograph was taken on 2th December 1962- the day before the main line platforms were taken out of use- and shows the general layout of the main line station. The concrete lamp standards were probably added in the 1950s. (H.C.Casserley)

73.   Taken on the same date but from the east of the High Level overbridge, we can see the bay platform (right), created in 1879 for terminating North London trains via Primrose Hill, and curving off to the left are the goods-only lines to Kew and Richmond of the former North & South Western Junction Railway. (H.C.Casserley)

74. By 1979, when this eastward view was taken, the 1890s building no longer served the main line station onto which it backed and the whole area was beginning to look dilapidated. The rather utilitarian porte-cochere erected in 1912 enabled passengers for the New Line to cross the bus road without exposure to the elements. (J.C.Gillham)

75. Further east along the approach road in the following year we can see some earlier buildings dating from the 1860s. Like the old booking office they were to have a further twenty years of life. In the distance are the massive cooling towers of Acton Lane power station, whilst the block to the right was a local authority nuclear bunker. (J.C.Gillham)

76.   The vast alterations caused by the 1960s electrification can be seen in this eastward 1999 shot from above the site of the old Main Line platforms. The West Coast Traincare Centre is to the left, with a Bakerloo train clattering away behind it, whilst to the right is the Perry Meyer scrapyard. (V. Mitchell)

77.   Passing now to the still-active New Station, opened on 15th June 1912, this 1963 photo gives us an overview of the platforms as seen from the old footbridge. The rear of the New Line booking office is seen beyond the New Station signal box, and in the background is a train at the High Level platform. At this point in time the nearest platform was numbered 12. (Stations UK)

78.   The New Station incorporated two bay platforms for terminating trains from Broad Street either via Hampstead Heath or via Primrose Hill. These services have long been phased out but one of the bays remains for use if required. In late 1964 it would appear the second bay has only just been taken out of use. New Line signalling was changed to colour light on 12th December 1988, the previous equipment having served since 1933. (J.C.Gillham)

79.   In 1979 the New Station signal box still stood opposite the down platform. A standard LNWR design, the box has since been demolished. A new signalling centre was built west of the station to control the DC lines northwards from South Hampstead. The main lines were brought under the control of Wembley Signalling Centre in January 2001. Northwards, line speeds were increased (fast from 90 to 125, slow 70 to 100mph) and some freight tracks upgraded for passengers. (J.C.Gillham)

80.   The New Line booking office is really a secondary entrance accessed via a passengers footpath from Harlesden High Street and is near the High Level platforms. Carried out in red brick with York Stone details it is in a style that we will become familiar with as we move further down the line. It had recently been renovated and reopened. (K.A.Scholey)

81.   This is the current main entrance, a new building erected in the Millenium Year, rather further down the approach road than the old version seen in picture 70. The exposed metal work carried out in bright colours makes it attractive and the lift is a useful addition. (K.A.Scholey)

82.   In 2001 the appearance of the platforms had altered somewhat. The new footbridge comes down almost in the middle of the platform area rather than at the end. To the left are the goods-only connecting lines up to the high level North London line, which were about to be electrified. The New Station has always been a pleasantly green area, but the buddleias impede photography. (K.A.Scholey)

84.   As our train leaves Willesden Junction we pass the Freightliner depot. In this 1967 view, taken not long after the opening of the depot, a Morris Goliath transporter crane is shifting a container from rail to road. The depot was built partly on the site of the old North Carriage Shed. (A.C.Ingram)

83.   In this 1993 shot a three-car class 313 unit, then the standard local train on the Euston-Watford line, ascends after passing under the goods-only line (to right) just west of the station. Built for the ex-Great Northern lines electrification in the mid-1970s, the 313s were transferred to the old North Western electric system a decade later. (M.Turvey)

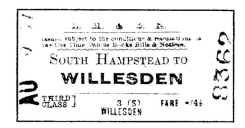

L. ... & ... R.
Issued subject to the conditions & regulations in the Company's Time Tables Books Bills & Notices.

SOUTH HAMPSTEAD TO

WILLESDEN

THIRD CLASS   3 (S)   FARE -/4½
WILLESDEN

WILLESDEN SHED

85. Willesden shed, first used in 1873, mostly housed locomotives for goods and local passenger work. This shot dates to around 1920 and shows a fine array of engines in steam ready for action. (R.M.Casserley coll.)

86.   In this grimmer post-war view, the shed has been considerably altered and the front section of roofing removed. With the exception of the tank engines for local goods use, the locomotives are markedly heavier. All the rolling stock stands in dirty contrast to the magnificently polished machines of the LNWR era view. (K.A.Scholey coll.)

87.   Two engines, including one of the famous Black Fives, are being prepared for use in around 1960, whilst the coaling plant, dating from the 1930s, looms in the background. (K.A.Scholey coll.)

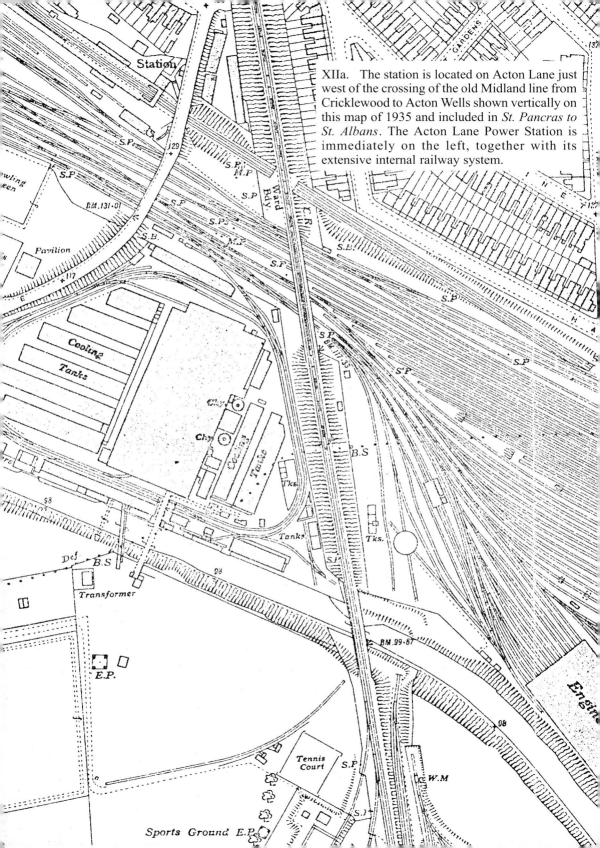

XIIa.   The station is located on Acton Lane just west of the crossing of the old Midland line from Cricklewood to Acton Wells shown vertically on this map of 1935 and included in *St. Pancras to St. Albans*. The Acton Lane Power Station is immediately on the left, together with its extensive internal railway system.

HARLESDEN

88.　　Looking east from the Acton Lane bridge in 1930, an express is seen rushing by on the fast lines while a line of coal wagons is shunted towards the engine sheds. The entrance to the Acton Lane power station is on the far right and the ex-Midland line crosses via the bridge. (Milepost 92½/R.S.Carpenter)

89.　　No. 5506, a "Patriot" class locomotive, leads a short Euston bound train in this 1934 view. The Patriots, or Baby Scots, were primarily used on medium distance express services on the West Coast main line from the 1920s to 1960s. In the background can be seen part of the Willesden classification yards. The New Line is off camera to the right. (H.F.Wheeller)

90.   Harlesden opened on 15th June 1912 and was very near the site of the first (1844-66) Willesden station. Extensive use of red brick and generous wooden canopies characterise the standard design for stations on this line. A 1938 Bakerloo train is leaving for the Elephant & Castle in this 1964 view. The footbridge has since been roofed. (J.C.Gillham)

NORTH OF HARLESDEN

91.   The line has now entered an extensive industrial area once characterised by numerous private sidings. This example served the McVities biscuit works off Waxlow Road just north of the station. Tasty smells still permeate trains as they pass this point. (K.A.Scholey coll.)

XIIb. There was a branch south to the Royal Agricultural Society's showground at Park Royal. It was intended to be a permanent site, but trains ran intermittently between 26th March and 5th July 1903. Passenger service appears to have been provided only during the show, from 13th June. It served the 1905 show and possibly the one in 1904. This map at 6ins to 1 mile shows the remains (centre) as "Twyford Abbey Sidings" and Park Royal being developed as an industrial estate. The name was derived from the last word of Twyford Abbey Estate and the first of the society. The LNWR's station name of Royal Showground was an inaccurate abbreviation. The main line is marked LMSR and the title is in full on the "New Line". The GWR is across the bottom. It also served the ground - see *Paddington to Princes Risborough*.

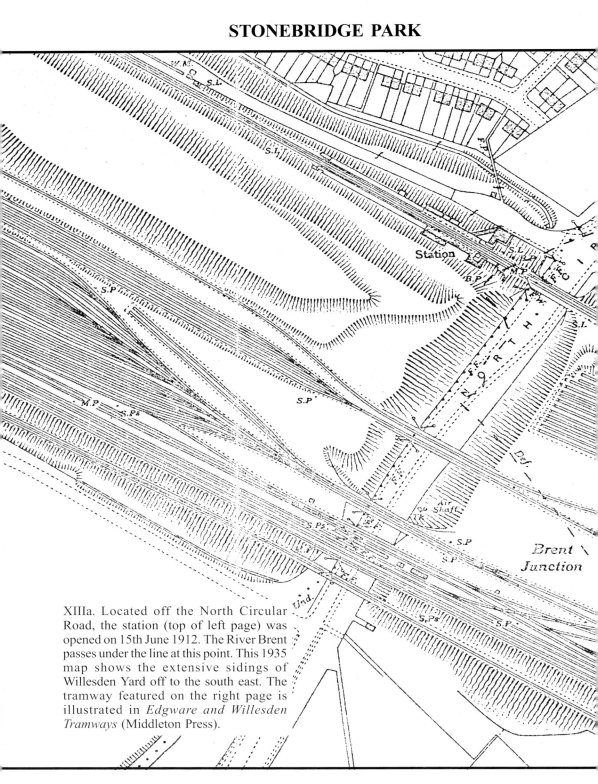

XIIIa. Located off the North Circular Road, the station (top of left page) was opened on 15th June 1912. The River Brent passes under the line at this point. This 1935 map shows the extensive sidings of Willesden Yard off to the south east. The tramway featured on the right page is illustrated in *Edgware and Willesden Tramways* (Middleton Press).

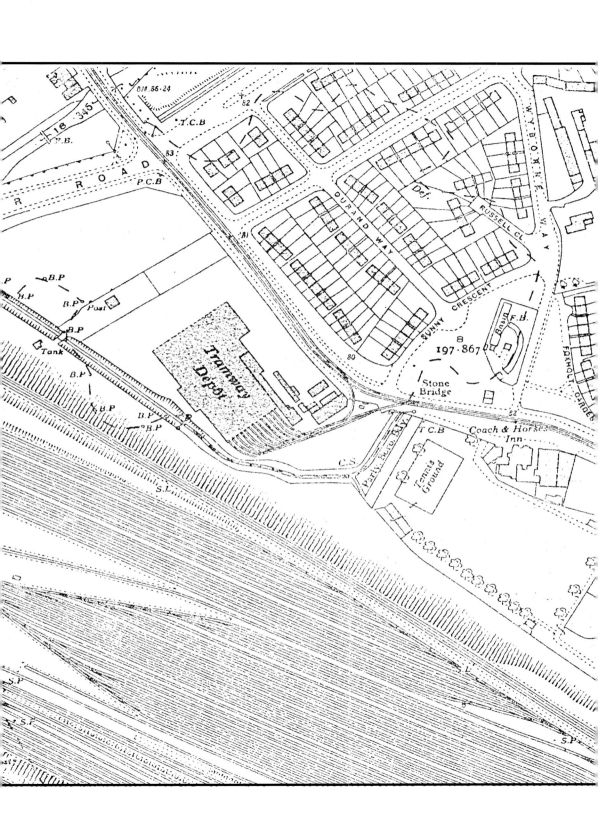

92. The station rests sleepily in the early Spring sunshine in 1973. The booking office building is the standard New Line type of red brick with stone details, although perhaps a little larger than elsewhere. (J.C.Gillham)

93. The platforms are perched on the embankment as can be seen in this 1976 view. The southbound building (left) dated from 1948 having been destroyed by fire three years earlier. (N.D.Mundy)

94.   The platform buildings were reconstructed to the form shown here in 2000. The new Royal Mail Distribution Centre can be seen behind the southbound train. It opened on 23rd September 1996 to accommodate seven platforms. The 65 dedicated trains would soon eliminate mail bags from London termini. (K.A.Scholey)

NORTH OF STONEBRIDGE PARK

95.   Stonebridge Park Power Station came online on 24th February 1916 and is seen here under construction two years earlier. The plant provided electricity for the whole of the LNWR's London electric system. When it closed on 30th July 1967, it was British Rail's last generating station. A tube depot is on the site now. (K.A.Scholey coll.)

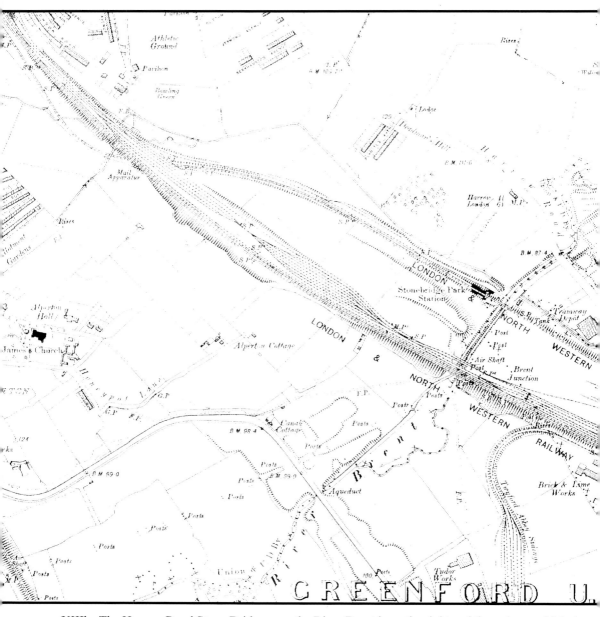

XIIIb. The Harrow Road Stone Bridge over the River Brent is on the right and the point at which the "New Line" passes under the original route is on the left. The recent developments described in captions 94 and 95 were created in spaces between the two routes shown on this 1912 revision at 6ins to 1 mile. Railfreight Distribution's new European Freight Operating Centre at Wembley was opened on 6th September 1993. It comprised 29 new sidings (with a total length of 10 miles), 70 sets of points and 60 signals, together with a signal control centre. The small Stonebridge Park goods yard is shown north-west of the station: goods traffic ceased in June 1951.

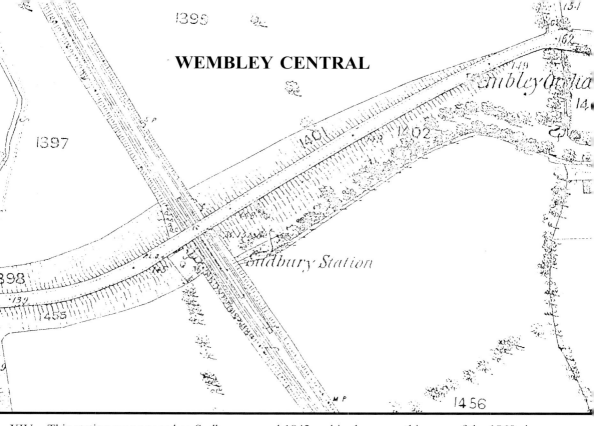

WEMBLEY CENTRAL

XIV.   This station was opened as Sudbury around 1842 and is shown on this map of the 1860s in virtually its original condition. At this time there had been little development in the area. It became Sudbury & Wembley on 1st May 1882, Wembley on 1st November 1910 and Wembley Central on 5th July 1948.

96.   This view is believed to date from around 1900 and shows the station as rebuilt in about 1875. On the left is the station masters house, which was demolished for the New Line platforms. The booking office is on the bridge over the fast lines. (Lens of Sutton)

XV.   What a contrast is the 1935 map! The whole area has been covered by housing and the railway is now a six track formation. The New Line has crossed under the main lines and is now served by the westernmost pair of platforms. Running across the page is the Great Central Railway's Neasden to South Ruislip line of 1906.

97. Around 1910 the exterior looked like this. The booking office is similar to the main line building at Willesden and may well date from the same period (early 1890s). The entrance to the goods yard is to the left. Goods traffic ceased on 4th January 1965. (K.A.Scholey coll.)

98. A new booking office erected in 1912 principally served the New Line platforms and is seen here in 1933. Although stylistically related to those seen so far, it has quite distinctive round arched windows. (London Transport)

99.   The New Line building was rather short lived and within a year or so of the previous picture had been pulled down. This 1934 shot shows an extensive range of advertising and the promise of a "handsome parade of shops". This view is to the left of the entrance. (K.A.Scholey coll.)

100.   The main subject of this 1961 picture is a LMS built electric train as used on the New Line between 1927 and 1962. These units differed from the earlier Oerlikon stock in having compartments with slam doors rather than end sliding doors. The New Line platform buildings were clearly quite similar to those found elsewhere. (F.Hornby)

101. The present exterior is carried out in a subdued Art Deco style as can be seen by this window detail. The booking office itself is set back from the shop frontage and includes a barrel-vaulted concourse and circular skylights. (K.A.Scholey)

102. The platforms were overlaid with a massive shopping block in the early 1960s and today are in a dark and none-too-welcoming concrete cavern. The 2½ acre concrete raft, required the support of 1000 piles, 400 of them being in the platforms. Class 501 units as shown here provided the Euston to Watford service between the late 1950s and 1985. The Southern Railway origins of the design may be noted. An innovation in 2002 was the provision of four trains per day to and from Gatwick Airport. (M.Turvey)

NORTH WEMBLEY

XVI. Our next stop was opened on 15th June 1912. The originally intended name for this station was East Lane after the thoroughfare it stands on. The small goods yard was located to the north of the road bridge and closed on 5th July 1965. Also on this 1935 map is the British Oxygen Company's private siding.

103.   The platforms are of the standard type as can be seen in this October 1964 view. In recent years in common with most of the older stations the waiting rooms have been bricked up. (N.D.Mundy)

104.   The booking office building is a typical example of its species and like its brethren is carried out in red brick with beige stone details. (K.A.Scholey)

SOUTH KENTON

South Kenton
Station

XVII. South Kenton was
the last new station to be
opened on the stretch of
line we are considering
and was only recently
completed when this map
was surveyed in 1935.
Opened on 3rd July 1933,
it serves the adjacent
Sudbury Court housing
estate.

The
Chestnuts

Chewing
Factor

105.   The island platform made the station a useful spot for observing the passing traffic. Here no. 45737 *Atlas*, a "Jubilee" class locomotive heads the 4.25pm Euston to Birmingham on 16th May 1959. The "Jubilees" were particularly suited to medium haul trips of this nature. (R.S.Carpenter)

106.   After speed, strength. A London bound freight headed by no. 48686, an 8F class locomotive, is next to pass. The 8F was the standard heavy goods engine used in late LMS and British Railways steam days on this line. (R.S.Carpenter)

107.   Today the station is entered via the subway seen in the foreground. The island platform is situated in an elevated position. Initially, as can be seen from the map, a footbridge led down directly into the booking office. (J.C.Gillham)

108.   The booking office, seen here on a rainy day in November 1979, was not an especially inviting sight. This station was different to the others on the New Line. (J.C.Gillham)

KENTON

XVIII. Our next halt is at another standard New Line station dating from 1912. Approached by a steep side road, the small goods yard was located on the other side of the main line and has been built over. It was closed on 3rd May 1965.

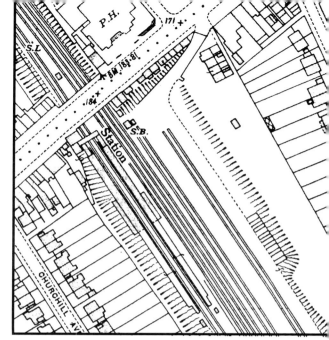

109. The street building here is almost identical to that at North Wembley as seen here on 5th June 1968. Between here and Harrow, the branch to Stanmore had turned north. The branch closed partially in 1952 and fully in 1964. (J.C.Gillham)

110. The platform buildings are again most typical of the New Line stations. This view was taken at the start of the long, hot Summer of 1976. (N.D.Mundy)

HARROW & WEALDSTONE

XIV. This 1935 map features seven platforms, a substantial footbridge and two street level buildings, one on Wealdstone High Street, the other from Marlborough Road (now Sandridge Close). Opened with the line on 20th July 1837, the station was originally the first stop out of Euston. Prior to 1897, when the suffix was added, it was named simply Harrow but seems to have always been locally known as Wealdstone. The goods yard (top) closed on 3rd April 1967. The Stanmore branch curves away at the lower border.

111.   This 1902 shot was taken looking south from the road bridge (known as The Bridge) adjacent to the station. On the left is the original No. 1 signal box, which controlled access to the Stanmore branch prior to the rebuilding of 1910-12. On the right is a terrace of typical LNWR railway cottages. (K.A.Scholey coll.)

112.   The Wealdstone entrance building, seen here in 1968, is the more well-known than its counterpart on the west side of the tracks. Built in 1912 and designed by Gerald Horsley it is an interesting if odd building, the finest feature being the striped clock tower. The bicycle shed block (far left) was demolished in 1977. (J.C.Gillham)

113.   The main line platforms are seen from the south in around 1934. The western two island platforms date from the rebuilding of 1912 and carry virtually identical buildings. The island serving the down fast and up DC local lines, on which we are standing, is much older dating back to 1875. Beneath the bridge can be seen the no. 1 signal box. (Stations UK)

114.   The terrible Harrow crash occurred at 8.18 am on 8th October 1952. A Perth-Euston express passed danger signals, probably due to fog, and crashed into a local train standing at platform 4. Another express (for Liverpool and Manchester) then ploughed into the wreckage. (H.C.Casserley)

115.   Three days later wreckage still litters the platforms. As can be seen here part of the footbridge was torn away. The damaged engine is no. 46242 *City of Glasgow*, which was later repaired. The engines leading the Liverpool/ Manchester express were not so lucky and both were scrapped. In all 112 people were killed in the worse peacetime rail disaster in Britain. (H.C.Casserley)

116.   Besides the overhead lines, which are not yet in use, little seems to have changed in this shot from thirty years later. However on closer inspection the details of canopies have been subtly altered, probably during repairs made after the Harrow crash. (J.C. Gillham)

117.   The New Line platforms (1 & 2) are to the south west of the station. The gables three quarters of the way along the canopy on platform 2 show where the old footbridge, pulled down during the reconstruction of 1912, used to stand. In October 1964 work was proceeding on the replacement road bridge. (J.C.Gillham)

118.   A wet day in 1979 gives us a nice overview of the New Line platforms (1 and 2). When the New Line was built in 1912 it took over the formation of the old fast lines which were diverted to the north-east. (J.C.Gillham)

119.   The Harrow side building, backing on to the New Line platforms, dates from 1875 and is a conventional Victorian station building (Italianate being the transport style). Built of yellow bricks with an overhanging slate roof it is a rather bleak old dinosaur. (K.A.Scholey)

120.   A train of 1972 Tube Stock (standard on the Bakerloo since 1986) is seen having left the reversing siding in the background for the return trip to the Elephant & Castle on 30th March 2002. However our journey stops here. (V.Mitchell)

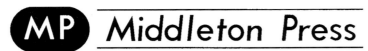

MP Middleton Press

Easebourne Lane, Midhurst, W Sussex. GU29 9AZ Tel: 01730 813169 Fax: 01730 812601
*If books are not available from your local transport stockist, order direct with cheque,
Visa or Mastercard, post free UK.*

BRANCH LINES
Branch Line to Allhallows
Branch Line to Alton
Branch Lines around Ascot
Branch Line to Ashburton
Branch Lines around Bodmin
Branch Line to Bude
Branch Lines around Canterbury
Branch Lines around Chard & Yeovil
Branch Line to Cheddar
Branch Lines around Cromer
Branch Lines to East Grinstead
Branch Lines of East London
Branch Lines to Effingham Junction
Branch Lines around Exmouth
Branch Lines to Falmouth, Helston & St. Ives
Branch Line to Fairford
Branch Lines around Gosport
Branch Line to Hayling
Branch Lines to Henley, Windsor & Marlow
Branch Line to Hawkhurst
Branch Lines around Huntingdon
Branch Line to Ilfracombe
Branch Line to Kingswear
Branch Line to Lambourn
Branch Lines to Launceston & Princetown
Branch Line to Looe
Branch Line to Lyme Regis
Branch Lines around Midhurst
Branch Line to Minehead
Branch Line to Moretonhampstead
Branch Lines to Newport
Branch Lines to Newquay
Branch Lines around North Woolwich
Branch Line to Padstow
Branch Lines around Plymouth
Branch Lines to Seaton and Sidmouth
Branch Lines around Sheerness
Branch Lines to Shrewsbury
Branch Line to Swanage *updated*
Branch Line to Tenterden
Branch Lines around Tiverton
Branch Lines to Torrington
Branch Line to Upwell
Branch Lines of West London
Branch Lines around Weymouth
Branch Lines around Wimborne
Branch Lines around Wisbech

NARROW GAUGE
Branch Line to Lynton
Branch Lines around Portmadoc 1923-46
Branch Lines around Porthmadog 1954-94
Branch Line to Southwold
Douglas to Port Erin
Douglas to Peel
Kent Narrow Gauge
Northern France Narrow Gauge
Romneyrail
Southern France Narrow Gauge
Sussex Narrow Gauge
Two-Foot Gauge Survivors
Vivarais Narrow Gauge

SOUTH COAST RAILWAYS
Ashford to Dover
Bournemouth to Weymouth
Brighton to Worthing
Eastbourne to Hastings
Hastings to Ashford
Portsmouth to Southampton
Ryde to Ventnor
Southampton to Bournemouth

SOUTHERN MAIN LINES
Basingstoke to Salisbury
Bromley South to Rochester
Crawley to Littlehampton
Dartford to Sittingbourne
East Croydon to Three Bridges
Epsom to Horsham
Exeter to Barnstaple
Exeter to Tavistock
Faversham to Dover
London Bridge to East Croydon
Orpington to Tonbridge
Tonbridge to Hastings
Salisbury to Yeovil
Sittingbourne to Ramsgate
Swanley to Ashford
Tavistock to Plymouth
Three Bridges to Brighton
Victoria to Bromley South
Victoria to East Croydon
Waterloo to Windsor
Waterloo to Woking
Woking to Portsmouth
Woking to Southampton
Yeovil to Exeter

EASTERN MAIN LINES
Barking to Southend
Ely to Kings Lynn
Ely to Norwich
Fenchurch Street to Barking
Ipswich to Saxmundham
Liverpool Street to Ilford
Saxmundham to Yarmouth
Tilbury Loop

WESTERN MAIN LINES
Didcot to Swindon
Ealing to Slough
Exeter to Newton Abbot
Newton Abbot to Plymouth
Newbury to Westbury
Paddington to Ealing
Paddington to Princes Risborough
Plymouth to St. Austell
Princes Risborough to Banbury
Reading to Didcot
Slough to Newbury
St. Austell to Penzance
Taunton to Exeter
Westbury to Taunton

MIDLAND MAIN LINES
Euston to Harrow & Wealdstone
St. Pancras to St. Albans

COUNTRY RAILWAY ROUTES
Abergavenny to Merthyr
Andover to Southampton
Bath to Evercreech Junction
Bournemouth to Evercreech Junction
Burnham to Evercreech Junction
Cheltenham to Andover
Croydon to East Grinstead
Didcot to Winchester
East Kent Light Railway
Fareham to Salisbury
Guildford to Redhill
Reading to Basingstoke
Reading to Guildford
Redhill to Ashford
Salisbury to Westbury
Stratford upon Avon to Cheltenham
Strood to Paddock Wood
Taunton to Barnstaple
Wenford Bridge to Fowey
Westbury to Bath
Woking to Alton
Yeovil to Dorchester

GREAT RAILWAY ERAS
Ashford from Steam to Eurostar
Clapham Junction 50 years of change
Festiniog in the Fifties
Festiniog in the Sixties
Festiniog 50 years of enterprise
Isle of Wight Lines 50 years of change
Railways to Victory 1944-46
Return to Blaenau 1970-82
SECR Centenary album
Talyllyn 50 years of change
Yeovil 50 years of change

LONDON SUBURBAN RAILWAYS
Caterham and Tattenham Corner
Charing Cross to Dartford
Clapham Jn. to Beckenham Jn.
Crystal Palace (HL) & Catford Loop
East London Line
Finsbury Park to Alexandra Palace
Holbourn Viaduct to Lewisham
Kingston and Hounslow Loops
Lewisham to Dartford
Lines around Wimbledon
London Bridge to Addiscombe
Mitcham Junction Lines
North London Line
South London Line
West Croydon to Epsom
West London Line
Willesden Junction to Richmond
Wimbledon to Beckenham
Wimbledon to Epsom

STEAMING THROUGH
Steaming through Cornwall
Steaming through the Isle of Wight
Steaming through Kent
Steaming through West Hants
Steaming through West Sussex

TRAMWAY CLASSICS
Aldgate & Stepney Tramways
Barnet & Finchley Tramways
Bath Tramways
Brighton's Tramways
Bristol's Tramways
Burton & Ashby Tramways
Camberwell & W.Norwood Tramways
Clapham & Streatham Tramways
Croydon's Tramways
Dover's Tramways
East Ham & West Ham Tramways
Edgware and Willesden Tramways
Eltham & Woolwich Tramways
Embankment & Waterloo Tramways
Enfield & Wood Green Tramways
Exeter & Taunton Tramways
Greenwich & Dartford Tramways
Hammersmith & Hounslow Tramways
Hampstead & Highgate Tramways
Hastings Tramways
Holborn & Finsbury Tramways
Ilford & Barking Tramways
Kingston & Wimbledon Tramways
Lewisham & Catford Tramways
Liverpool Tramways 1. Eastern Routes
Liverpool Tramways 2. Southern Routes
Liverpool Tramways 3. Northern Routes
Maidstone & Chatham Tramways
Margate to Ramsgate
North Kent Tramways
Norwich Tramways
Reading Tramways
Seaton & Eastbourne Tramways
Shepherds Bush & Uxbridge Tramway
Southend-on-sea Tramways
Southwark & Deptford Tramways
Stamford Hill Tramways
Twickenham & Kingston Tramways
Victoria & Lambeth Tramways
Waltham Cross & Edmonton Tramway
Walthamstow & Leyton Tramways
Wandsworth & Battersea Tramways

TROLLEYBUS CLASSICS
Croydon Trolleybuses
Derby Trolleybuses
Hastings Trolleybuses
Huddersfield Trolleybuses
Maidstone Trolleybuses
Portsmouth Trolleybuses
Woolwich & Dartford Trolleybuses

WATERWAY ALBUMS
Kent and East Sussex Waterways
London to Portsmouth Waterway
West Sussex Waterways

MILITARY BOOKS
Battle over Portsmouth
Battle over Sussex 1940
Bombers over Sussex 1943-45
Bognor at War
Military Defence of West Sussex
Military Signals from the South Coast
Secret Sussex Resistance
Surrey Home Guard

OTHER RAILWAY BOOKS
Index to all Middleton Press stations
Industrial Railways of the South-East
South Eastern & Chatham Railways
London Chatham & Dover Railway
War on the Line (SR 1939-45)

BIOGRAPHY
Garraway Father & Son